PRAY FOR OUR LEADERS

118TH CONGRESS

ED GRUBER

Copyright © 2023 ED GRUBER

All Rights Reserved.
Printed in the U.S.A.

Published by Two Penny Publishing
850 E Lime Street #266
Tarpon Springs, FL 34688
TwoPennyPublishing.com
info@twopennypublishing.com

No part of this publication may be reproduced, distributed, or transmitted in any form or by any means, including photocopying, recording, or other electronic or mechanical methods, without the prior written permission of the publisher, except in the case of brief quotations embodied in critical reviews and certain other noncommercial uses permitted by copyright law.

For permission requests and ordering information, email the publisher at: info@twopennypublishing.com

Scripture quotations marked (ESV) are taken from The ESV® Bible (The Holy Bible, English Standard Version®), copyright © 2001 by Crossway, a publishing ministry of Good News Publishers. Used by permission. All rights reserved.

Scripture quotations marked (NIV) are taken from the Holy Bible, New International Version®, NIV®. Copyright © 1973, 1978, 1984, 2011 by Biblica, Inc.™ Used by permission of Zondervan. All rights reserved worldwide. www.zondervan.comThe "NIV" and "New International Version" are trademarks registered in the United States Patent and Trademark Office by Biblica, Inc.™

"Black vector map of the United States on white background free vector" graphic by Vecteezy.com

"White background of world map with line art design free vector" graphic by Vecteezy.com

ISBN: 978-1-950995-95-0

Library of Congress Control Number: 2023906530

FIRST EDITION

For more information about the author or to book him for your next event or media interview, please contact his representative at: info@twopennypublishing.com

> Two Penny Publishing is a partnership publisher of a variety of genres. We help first-time and seasoned authors share their stories, passion, knowledge, and experiences that help others grow and learn. Please visit our website: TwoPennyPublishing.com if you would like us to consider your manuscript or book idea for publishing.

Introduction

DECEMBER 2022

When "Pray for Our Leaders" was released in early 2021, the response was humbling, to say the least. I spoke at churches, in small groups, and with a wide array of individuals. Not a single person said or suggested that praying for our elected leaders seemed like a bad idea. Further, no one (at least to my face) said that praying was a waste of time. I know for a fact that people took up the challenge and began to pray for our national elected leaders by name. I know this because many people have told me so. I guess they all could have been lying but, somehow, I doubt that. So that leads to an interesting question.

What if God orchestrated the 2022 elections; almost like it was planned with a purpose?

If that assertion is accurate, then approximately 50% of the electorate/public will likely become very frustrated and discouraged while the very same result will make the "other side" ecstatic.

In the many conversations I have had about *Pray for Our Leaders*, people routinely ask, "Why did you do this?" That question drives me into many interesting places. I usually answer with something like, "Why hasn't anyone else done this before?" Then, of course, my own mind kicks in and re-forms the question.

Why did YOU write this? Who do you think YOU are?

My wife and I have two wonderful children who are twenty and eighteen. In the fall of 2016, while candidates Donald Trump and Hillary Clinton were engaging in the presidential debates, my daughter (then fourteen) and I were watching one. Afterward there was the post-debate analysis on all of the normal networks. I was trying to be open-minded and absorb different perspectives, so I was toggling between Fox News and MSNBC. The difference in conclusions, not surprisingly, were stark. After flipping back and forth between the two channels for only a few minutes, my inquisitive daughter looked over at me and simply asked, "Are they even talking about the same thing?"

I was frozen by her question.

My eyes were instantly opened to a sad fact: our national consciousness was deeply damaged and hurting. News organizations function to earn money. They do so by attracting and holding viewers so advertisers can reach their targeted masses. The drastically opposing explanations and interpretations of that debate were designed to cater to each network's viewer base. If those bases were so vastly different, what did that say about the state of our nation?

Wheels began to turn. A book was born. However, it was far more than just a book. I quickly realized that my own prayer life was about to embark on a radical, new, and uncomfortable journey.

2022 was an incredible year on many fronts. There was and continues to be widespread fear about the economy, the stock market, the housing market, interest rates, and dozens of other legitimately troubling threats. On top of that, throw in another national election. As I type these words, we are only a few weeks beyond the mid-term elections that decided control of congress. Also, thirty-six states held elections for governor on November 8, 2022. Even through Thanksgiving week, many congressional contests as well as governorships had not been finalized. Not surprisingly, just like the 2020 presidential election cycle, emotions ran and are running extremely high.

While many media heavy weights in 2020 often uttered phrases like, "This is the most important election in our lifetime," (just like they did in 2016), we are seeing an even more elevated profile of the importance of the recent elections. To say the nation is polarized over politics is an intense understatement. Disagreements previously solved over a cup of coffee at the end of adjacent driveways have morphed into relational wedges never to be repaired.

If one watches almost any national news broadcast, an unsettling reality quickly emerges. There is a general tendency to create an "us and them" scenario. Our largely two-party political system has created this framework. Over the past several years, demonization of the other side has proven to be a well-traveled and worn path to popularity. We seem to have gone from a competitive to a much more confrontational political environment.

The "other side" gets labeled racist or fascist or socialist or communist. Those labels give the user an odd degree of permission to put everyone with whom he or she disagrees into a denigrated group; all possessing the same horrible characteristics that must be avoided or stamped out at all costs.

Where is the church? Where are the Christians? Where are people who understand that there is more "middle ground" out there that any public opinion seems to want?

Where are the peacemakers?

That is not meant to be a series of rhetorical questions. As I have read, listened to, and thought deeply about opinions, a curious truth seems to have emerged. The loudest voice or the most controversial stance gets the "likes," "shares," or "follows." As a result, that loud voice gets to drive the initial narrative. Not because it's the best or even the most logical. Oftentimes, it's because the other side simply tires of the argument and retreats.

The megaphone wins.

Following is an excerpt from "The Christian Culture Survival Guide" by Matthew Paul Turner. This book, published in 2004, mostly pokes fun at Christian stereotypes but there is a serious tone in the latter section of the book.

> "Sadly, most Christian denominations have spent the last 2000 years trying to define Jesus in human terms, attempting to compress His teachings into more digestible tidbits. But we were never meant to *digest* the teachings of Jesus; we were meant to live them out. Today, we have such a limited understanding of how truly radical Jesus is. We're relying too heavily on our Christian books, Christian music, and TV evangelists to guide our thinking. We wear our silly Jesus

T-shirts and jewelry and hang our Bible verse plaques and we think we are proclaiming the name of Christ. We go to festivals, revivals, and church functions and call it true fellowship. We put "Jesus Saves" on a billboard and think we've done something really miraculous. We sing a few praise songs and listen to a man or woman lecture on scripture, and we think we've experienced worship. We stand outside a courthouse and picket the removal of The Ten Commandments and we think we're fighting the good fight. We hold up our signs reading "God Hates Fags" and we truly believe we are helping to awaken a perverted culture. We join the "Christian" club and separate ourselves from the world, and the world still sits on the outside, dying for someone to demonstrate what it means to believe."[1]

What if the people of God boldly prayed for our elected leaders without regard for politics? Might "the church" start to look different than "the world?" Do you think that if we selflessly prayed for those in political office that we might be viewed as different, as if on a different mission than the normal news cycles regularly suggest?

The 2022 national election cycle generated at least as much distrust as the 2020 cycle did, if not more. As much as the previous statement is proven stunningly true each moment across seemingly the entire internet in news feeds and social media postings, a very simple truth keeps creeping to the surface.

As my last living Aunt (thank you Aunt Pam) said to me recently, "We were made for such a time as this."

Our Father in Heaven wants us to engage, not retreat. God has armed each of His followers with a Bible full of promises. He will NEVER leave or forsake us. The more uncertain the political landscape seems, the more we should pray. Pray for one another. Pray for our families and friends. Pray for our Pastors and church leaders. On the national political front, pray for the men and women who God has selected to serve in their roles.

---

[1] Turner, M. P. (2004). *The Christian Culture Survival Guide: The Misadventures of an Outsider on the Inside.* Relevant Media Group.

For many years in public evangelical circles, 2 Chronicles 7:14 (ESV) gets quoted as a rallying cry for revival in our nation. It's a great verse and probably is printed on many plaques in pastor's offices and church leader's family rooms.

The verse is as follows:

> "If my people who are called by my name humble themselves, and pray, and seek my face, and turn from their wicked ways, then I will hear from heaven and will forgive their sin and heal their land."

There is so much in that great Old Testament verse. Do you feel the energy? It's easy to see the power of speaking this as an inspirational, motivational call to action, precisely as it was originally intended.

Regardless of one's political alignment, it's clear that our land is anything but healed. As you read this passage, you'll notice that it's a bold if/then statement. If A happens, then B will follow. Look at the sequence of promises and the progression that must take place for the healing of the land. In order to expect healing, national sin would have to be forgiven. In order for national sin to be forgiven, God would have to have heard from Heaven. In order for God to have heard from Heaven, we would have had to have turned from our wicked ways. In order for us to have turned from our wicked ways, we would have previously been seeking God's face. Before seeking God's face, we would have been praying. Even prior to praying, we, the people of God, would have humbled ourselves.

Humble ourselves. Humble myself.

It seems to me that when we pray decidedly for other people (without asking God to throw something in for ourselves), that is among the humblest things we can do. Think about what may actually happen if we as a nation regularly prayed for our elected officials. I don't mean to quickly sneak in a prayer like a text message to God. I mean heartfelt, sincere, pleading prayers for the people who God has installed in our various branches of government.

As recent political temper tantrums have vividly displayed, we have strayed as a nation. Entrenched career politicians invoke religious precepts as an afterthought or as a weapon to diminish their opponent while hypocritically not living up to the standard that they accuse another of violating.

I certainly have political opinions, just like everyone else does. However, this is in no way a political or opinion book. So you can relax with the understanding that you did not get "duped" into buying a Republican, Democratic, Conservative, Progressive, or whatever-other-tribal-label-may-come-to-mind book.

Take a deep breath. Now take another.

This is not going to be a "bait and switch."

Please notice what has *not* been mentioned: party affiliations. Before you allow yourself to mentally drift to, "He's probably a [fill in the blank]" or "He sounds like my co-worker who always votes [fill in the blank here too]," stop and think. *Really* think.

What has happened to civil conversations with people who hold different political opinions?

I want to address and emphasize the "why" and "how" behind this endeavor.

Why

I am a follower of Jesus Christ. Many variations of that label exist both inside and outside the church. Some like to say "Christian." Others don't go that far and use more generic adjectives like "religious" or "spiritual." Yet others walk into a more cerebral arena and call themselves "theists." I am certain there are many other self-imposed adjectives that attempt to capture a basic acknowledgement of God's (or a higher power's) existence.

Please don't misunderstand. I am not in any way diminishing where you might be on your own spiritual journey-or if you are even on a spiritual journey at all. My hunch is that if you are reading this book, you at least have some inkling that there is a God and He is involved in the affairs of humanity as well as in individual lives. Furthermore, you likely have something going on deep inside that has been speaking to you—challenging you to reach and grow.

You might be in a Sunday School class and this seemed like a timely topic. After all, praying for our leaders seems like a wise thing to do, so here you sit.

How

I assembled a very simple guide so we all can pray for our representatives, senators, and national executive leaders, regardless of who you voted for.

On the pages that follow are several lists. One is the President and his cabinet. Following that is a state-by-state list of national elected officials who are in Washington on our behalf. These people need our prayers. As the people of God, we need to step up and boldly pray for these leaders who were installed by God. Again, take careful notice of what is missing from these lists: political party affiliation. That is not a lazy oversight. Rather, that is very much by design so that we pray for each person as a man or woman who is made in the image of Almighty God and is serving our great nation and the voters who elected them.

Clearly, some people in these pages did not get your vote. Some people, in your view, should never be allowed to be near leadership of any kind. For most every politician listed, there is someone else who also ran an exhausting and expensive campaign. Family time was sacrificed. Careers were put on hold or entirely redirected.

But they lost; some by incredibly small margins.

Just because "your person" did not win, you should not lose interest. God merely had plans that did not line up with theirs (or yours) at this moment in time.

As we did in 2020, we are calling for an uprising of prayerful voices for those who God has installed in their positions of power and influence. Ephesians 6:12 (ESV) reminds us who we are really pitted against. Spoiler alert: it's not our former friend who voted differently.

> "For we do not wrestle against flesh and blood, but against the rulers, against the authorities, against the cosmic powers over this present darkness, against the spiritual forces of evil in the heavenly places."

As we usher in the 118th Congress in early 2023, we need to pray with new focus and urgency for God to be sought and found by our political leaders. Let's pray that God inspires the daily discourse and supernaturally moves the hearts of these leaders in unmistakable and eternal ways.

What do you think might happen if the collective body of God's people *constantly* prayed for our elected and appointed leaders? If we cry out to God on their behalf for wisdom in their policy making and negotiations, do we as God's people think—*really believe*—that God would move? What if daily around America there were thousands or millions of people lifting our leaders to our heavenly Father and begging for God's wisdom to invade the political process for His purposes and His glory?

I say, "Let's find out."

After each list is an area for notes. Jot down dates of when you pray and, most importantly, how God answers those prayers. Let's believe in God to move in supernatural ways in the hearts of these leaders He has installed.

I pray for God's rich and clear blessing on you and yours. Thank you for joining me on this worthy and much-needed journey.

President and Cabinet

PRESIDENT
Joseph R. Biden Jr.

VICE PRESIDENT
Kamala Harris

SECRETARY OF STATE
Antony Blinken

SECRETARY OF VETERANS AFFAIRS
Denis McDonough

SECRETARY OF THE TREASURY
Dr. Janet Yellen

SECRETARY OF HOMELAND SECURITY
Alejandro Mayorkas

SECRETARY OF DEFENSE
Lloyd Austin

ADMINISTRATOR OF THE ENVIRONMENTAL PROTECTION AGENCY
Michael Regan

ATTORNEY GENERAL
Merrick Garland

DIRECTOR OF OFFICE OF MANAGEMENT AND BUDGET
Shalanda Young

SECRETARY OF THE INTERIOR
Deb Haaland

DIRECTOR OF NATIONAL INTELLIGENCE
Avril Haines

SECRETARY OF AGRICULTURE Tom Vilsack	**US TRADE REPRESENTATIVE** Katherine Tai
SECRETARY OF COMMERCE Gina Raimondo	**US AMBASSADOR TO THE UNITED NATIONS** Linda Thomas-Greenfield
SECRETARY OF LABOR Marty Walsh	**CHAIR OF THE COUNCIL OF ECONOMIC ADVISORS** Dr. Cecilia Rouse
SECRETARY OF HEALTH AND HUMAN SERVICES Xavier Becerra	**ADMINISTRATOR OF THE SMALL BUSINESS ADMINISTRATION** Isabel Guzman
SECRETARY OF HOUSING AND URBAN DEVELOPMENT Marcia Fudge	**PRESIDENTIAL SCIENCE ADVISER/DIRECTOR OF THE OFFICE OF SCIENCE AND TECHNOLOGY POLICY** Dr. Arati Prabhakar
SECRETARY OF TRANSPORTATION Pete Buttigieg	**CHIEF OF STAFF** Jeff Zients
SECRETARY OF ENERGY Jennifer Granholm	**SECRETARY OF EDUCATION** Dr. Miguel Cardona

> "For the LORD gives *wisdom*; from His mouth come *knowledge* and *understanding*."
>
> Proverbs 2:6 (ESV)

Father in Heaven, please guide our president and his cabinet. Help them to acknowledge that the only source of true wisdom is You. We beg you, God, on behalf of these leaders WHO YOU HAVE PERMITTED to be in their positions, that they would be humble and seek Your perfect wisdom daily. Help them all to lead well. Please protect their families and help them to never forget that You love them and that they are all part of Your perfect plan. Amen.

Alabama

US REPRESENTATIVES
Robert B. Aderholt

Jerry L. Carl

Barry Moore

Gary J. Palmer

Mike D. Rogers

Terri A. Sewell

Dale Strong

US SENATORS
Katie Boyd Britt

Tommy Tuberville

> "Therefore, you kings, be **wise**; be warned, you rulers of the earth.
> **Serve** the LORD with fear and **celebrate** His rule with trembling."
>
> Psalm 2:10-11 (NIV)

We lift these elected leaders of Alabama to You, LORD. Grant them all insight and wisdom far beyond their human abilities. Help them see, increasingly each day, that the work they do is ultimately for the King of Kings… for Your divine purposes. Help them put selfish ambitions aside and fix their eyes on You as they take up Your work each day. Amen.

Alaska

US REPRESENTATIVE
Mary Sattler Peltola

US SENATORS
Lisa Murkowski
Dan Sullivan

"The King's *heart* is a stream of water in the hand of the LORD; He *turns* it wherever He will."

Proverbs 21:1 (ESV)

Father in heaven, we pray for these elected leaders from Alaska. We know they are serving because You want them there. Please guide their thinking and help them to see that You are ALWAYS available and ALWAYS faithful. If they call to You, You will answer and help them.

Thank you for your faithfulness and patience with Your people. Amen.

American Samoa

DELEGATE
Aumua Amata Coleman Radewagen

> "The LORD has established His ***throne*** in the heavens, and His ***kingdom*** rules over all."
>
> Psalm 103:19 (ESV)

Almighty God, You do in fact rule over all. Thank You for Your grace and autonomy to establish a system of government that gives a voice to all citizens. We pray for the delegate in American Samoa. We ask for boldness and humility despite being only a single voice, that You would make her understand that many times throughout history, generational movements were started by a single voice. We ask that Your will be done through this single voice. Amen.

Arizona

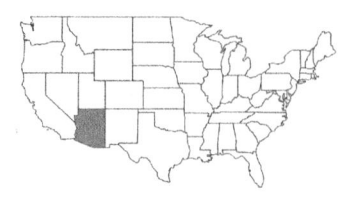

US REPRESENTATIVES
Andy Biggs

Juan Ciscomani

Elijah Crane

Ruben Gallego

Paul A. Gosar

Raul M. Grijalva

Debbie Lesko

David Schweikert

Greg Stanton

US SENATORS
Mark Kelly

Kyrsten Sinema

> "Many are the plans in the mind of a man, but it is the *purpose* of the LORD that will **stand**."
>
> Proverbs 19:21 (ESV)

Creator God, please guide these representative leaders from Arizona. Guide their thinking, conversations, and policy-making efforts. Help them lead with You in mind as well as the people they represent. Help them always see the bigger picture and understand that what they are doing in congress can do great things for a lot of people. Amen.

Arkansas

US REPRESENTATIVES
Eric A. (Rick) Crawford
J. French Hill
Bruce Westerman
Steve Womack

US SENATORS
John Boozman
Tom Cotton

> "May he judge Your people with *righteousness* and your poor with *justice*."
>
> Psalm 72:2 (ESV)

LORD, the responsibility of leading is immense. As these leaders show up to work each day, please keep their focus on You. The people they have the honor of leading deserve integrity, honesty, and strength in their elected leaders. Empower these leaders from Arkansas with the stamina and ability to lead well. Amen.

California

US REPRESENTATIVES

Pete Aguilar
Nanette Diaz Barragan
Ami Bera
Julia Brownley
Ken Calvert
Salud O. Carbajal
Judy Chu
J. Luis Correa
Jim Costa
Tony Cardenas
Mark DeSaulnier
John Duarte
Anna G. Eshoo
John Garamendi
Mike Garcia
Robert Garcia
Jimmy Gomez
Josh Harder
Jared Huffman
Darrell E. Issa
Sara Jacobs
Sydney Kamlager-Dove
Ro Khanna
Kevin Kiley
Young Kim
Doug LaMalfa
Barbara Lee
Mike Levin
Ted Lieu
Zoe Lofgren
Doris O. Matsui
Kevin McCarthy
Tom McClintock
Kevin Mullin
Grace F. Napolitano
Jay Obernolte
Jimmy Panetta
Nancy Pelosi
Scott H. Peters
Katie Porter
Raul Ruiz
Linda Sanchez
Adam B. Schiff
Brad Sherman
Michelle Steel
Eric Swalwell
Mark Takano
Mike Thompson
Norma J. Torres
David G. Valadao
Juan Vargas
Maxine Waters

US SENATORS

Dianne Feinstein
Alex Padilla

> "By Me kings reign, and rulers decree what is *just*.
> By Me princes rule, and nobles, all who ***govern justly***."
>
> Proverbs 8:15-16 (ESV)

Merciful and Mighty God, Your children, Your created men and women elected these willing leaders in California. Father, You created each of them in Your image for Your purposes. We pray that Your wisdom and insights would fill each mind and that they would grasp the great weight and responsibility that they each hold. Help them not to be driven by self-interests or lust for power. Rather, that they would fully embrace their roles in leading Your people with purpose beyond anything they can imagine. Amen.

Colorado

US REPRESENTATIVES
Lauren Boebert
Ken Buck
Yadira Caraveo
Jason Crow
Diana DeGette
Doug Lamborn
Joe Neguse
Brittany Pettersen

US SENATORS
Michael F. Bennet
John W. Hickenlooper

*"**Humble** yourselves before the LORD, and He will lift you up."*

James 4:10 (NIV)

Father, as we can all see in the media, seemingly on a daily basis, there is a huge amount of self-serving and self-centeredness among our elected leaders. We pray for their humility. We pray that You remind them why they are really in office… to serve Your purposes. We pray specifically for these leaders from Colorado. Help them to see that their roles as Representatives and Senators are a noble calling and You deserve their best and most selfless efforts.

Thank you, LORD, for your faithfulness in ALWAYS hearing our prayers. Amen.

Connecticut

US REPRESENTATIVES
Joe Courtney
Rosa L. DeLauro
Jahana Hayes
James A. Himes
John B. Larson

US SENATORS
Richard Blumenthal
Christopher Murphy

> "Not so with you. Instead, whoever wants to become great among you must be your ***servant***."
>
> Matthew 20:26 (NIV)

LORD, as we have seen over the past several years, the attitude among our politicians is that they are "over" us and are somehow to be revered as bigger than life. In Your supernatural kindness, would You remind these leaders that they should be serving and looking for ways to serve the people rather than positioning themselves for power and influence? Thank You for your grace and patience with us. Amen.

Delaware

US REPRESENTATIVES
Lisa Blunt Rochester

US SENATORS
Thomas R. Carper
Christopher A. Coons

"Do nothing out of selfish ambition or vain conceit. Rather, in *humility* value others above yourself."

Philippians 2:3 (NIV)

Almighty God, when You spoke the universe into existence, You saw this very moment. You saw how our national politics would look. Father, help these leaders from Delaware lean into Your Word so they can help build policy and legislation that honors You. As Philippians 2:3 directs, guide these elected leaders to do their work in such a way that they value others above themselves. Amen.

District of Columbia

DELEGATE
Eleanor Holmes Norton

*"Let us not become weary in doing **good**, for at the proper time we will reap a **harvest** if we do not give up."*

Galatians 6:9 (NIV)

LORD God, from the founding of our country, Your hand has been on the formation and maintenance of our government. We are a blessed people. Guide us to return to principles that were clearly important to people who ventured out in faith to build a new nation called America. One voice can spark and lead tremendous change. Please help the Delegate from District of Columbia lead well with Your guidance and inspiration. Amen.

Florida

US REPRESENTATIVES

Aaron Bean
Gus Bilirakis
Vern Buchanan
Kat Cammack
Kathy Castor
Sheila Cherfilus-McCormick
Mario Diaz-Balart
Byron Donalds
Neal P. Dunn
Lois Frankel
C. Scott Franklin
Maxwell Frost
Matt Gaetz
Carlos A. Giminez
Laurel Lee

Anna Paulina Luna
Brian J. Mast
Cory Mills
Jared Moskowitz
Bill Posey
John H. Rutherford
Maria Elvira Salazar
Darren Soto
W. Gregory Steube
Michael Waltz
Debbie Wasserman Schultz
Daniel Webster
Frederica S. Wilson

US SENATORS

Marco Rubio
Rick Scott

"So in everything, do to **others** what you would have them do to you, for this sums up the Law and the Prophets."

Matthew 7:12 (NIV)

LORD, Your Word is timeless. It's always relevant and helpful. In our current political climate, we pray the words in Matthew 7:12 would inspire these elected leaders from Florida and all of us to simply be better... every day. Help them in their various meetings and committees to ALWAYS treat others as they would want to be treated. As they consider policy and legislation, remind them who they are truly working for.... the Creator God of the universe who has entrusted them with the leadership of others. May that truth guide them each day. Amen.

Georgia

US REPRESENTATIVES
Rick W. Allen
Sanford D. Bishop Jr.
Earl L. (Buddy) Carter
Andrew S. Clyde
Mike Collins
A. Drew Ferguson IV
Marjorie Taylor Greene
Henry C. (Hank) Johnson Jr.
Barry Loudermilk
Lucy McBath
Richard McCormick
Austin Scott
David Scott
Nikema Williams

US SENATORS
Jon Ossoff
Raphael G. Warnock

"He must become *greater*; I must become *less*."

John 3:30 (NIV)

Father in Heaven, You are powerfully residing on Your throne. You are King forever. LORD, we acknowledge Your power and rightful position. Please forgive us for our attempts to install ourselves, our politicians, our president, or celebrities in the place that only You should occupy. LORD, please guide the national political leaders from Georgia to always remember they are in their roles ONLY because You allowed it and You have noble work for them to do. Amen.

Guam

DELEGATE
James Moylan

"If a ruler listens to falsehood, all his officials will be wicked."

Proverbs 29:12 (ESV)

Father, we have seen in recent times political leaders being exposed for lying and deception. As You know, we now have "fact-checkers" that supposedly check the validity of a particular statement. The political climate has become deeply contentious and distrustful. LORD, please guide the Delegate from Guam to always seek and defend what is true. Thank you, God, for being intimately involved in the affairs of each day. Amen.

Hawaii

US REPRESENTATIVES
Ed Case
Jill N. Tokuda

US SENATORS
Mazie K. Hirono
Brian Schatz

> "Whoever exalts himself will be humbled, and whoever ***humbles*** himself will be ***exalted***."
>
> Matthew 23:12 (ESV)

LORD, this verse models what true leadership was intended to be. We have twisted and perverted what You intended real leadership to look like. Please forgive us. Father, please guide the elected officials from Hawaii to humbly serve You and their state. In their policy-making, guide them to see Your principles and purposes rather than their own or the loudest cries on the internet. We know that Your timing is perfect. We thank you for the ability to come before You and pray. Amen.

Idaho

US REPRESENTATIVES
Russ Fulcher
Michael K. Simpson

US SENATORS
Mike Crapo
James E. Risch

"Keep your *heart* with all vigilance, for from it flow the springs of *life*."

Proverbs 4:23 (ESV)

Heavenly Father, thank You for this great nation and the freedoms You have allowed to survive here so far. We lift up these elected leaders from Idaho. LORD, help them watch over their hearts and lead with graciousness and humility. Also, Father, may they never forget that their position in leadership is ONLY POSSIBLE because of You, and You are watching. Thank You for Your patience and Your perfect plan. Amen.

Illinois

US REPRESENTATIVES
Mike Bost
Nikki Budzinski
Sean Casten
Danny K. Davis
Bill Foster
Jesus G. (Chuy) Garcia
Jonathan Jackson
Robin L. Kelly
Raja Krishnamoorthi
Darin LaHood
Mary E. Miller
Mike Quigley
Delia Ramirez
Janice D. Schakowsky
Bradley Scott Schneider
Eric Sorensen
Lauren Underwood

US SENATORS
Tammy Duckworth
Richard J. Durbin

"Let what you say be *simply* 'Yes' or 'No'; anything more than this comes from evil."

Matthew 5:37 (ESV)

LORD God, as simple as these words are, why are they so difficult to consistently put into practice? LORD, we confidently ask for Your help for these elected officials from Illinois to take these words seriously and work hard each day to let their *yes'* be yes and their *no's* be no. Simply put, guide them to lead and govern with honesty, simplicity, and transparency. We boldly ask knowing that You hear our prayer, and You will definitely answer. Amen.

Indiana

US REPRESENTATIVES
James R. Baird
Jim Banks
Larry Bucshon
Andre Carson
Erin Houchin
Frank J. Mrvan
Greg Pence
Victoria Spartz
Rudy Yakym

US SENATORS
Mike Braun
Todd Young

"for *dominion* belongs to the LORD and He rules over the *nations*."

Psalm 22:28 (NIV)

Father, we kneel before You as our one true King. Thank You for Your grace and patience. We lift these national leaders elected from Indiana. Please guide them to lead with boldness knowing that their service is to You and for accomplishing Your divine purposes. When they interact with other politicians, help them to craft and promote policy and relationships that benefit our nation and our local communities in a way that honors You. Amen.

Iowa

US REPRESENTATIVES
Randy Feenstra
Ashley Hinson
Mariannette Miller-Meeks
Zachary Nunn

US SENATORS
Joni Ernst
Chuck Grassley

"Both *riches* and *honor* come from You, and You rule over all. In Your hand are *power* and *might*, and in Your hand it is to make great and to give strength to all. And now we thank you, our God, and *praise* Your glorious name."

1 Chronicles 29:12-13 (ESV)

LORD, what a powerful prayer that King David offered in this great passage of Your Word. As we pray for the elected leaders of Iowa, we humbly ask that You speak and work through them in their daily tasks. Help them to always remember that the work that You have for them is noble and honorable; despite how it has been portrayed in recent years. Help them and us find our way back to You as the rightful leader of our great nation. Amen.

_____
_____
_____
_____
_____
_____
_____
_____
_____

Kansas

US REPRESENTATIVES
Sharice Davids
Ron Estes
Jake LaTurner
Tracey Mann

US SENATORS
Roger W. Marshall
Jerry Moran

> "For a man's *ways* are before the eyes of the LORD, and he ponders all his *paths*."
>
> Proverbs 5:21 (ESV)

LORD God, we humbly ask for Your blessing and guidance for the elected leaders from Kansas. Help them look to You first as they meet to conduct the nation's political business. As the Proverb declares, everything we all do is clearly visible to You every moment of every day. We pray that these leaders lead with this sober fact in mind. Amen.

Kentucky

US REPRESENTATIVES
Andy Barr

James Comer

Brett Guthrie

Thomas Massie

Morgan McGarvey

Harold Rogers

US SENATORS
Mitch McConnell

Rand Paul

"Come and see what God has done: He is *awesome* in His deeds toward the children of man. He turned the sea into dry land; they passed through the river on foot. There did we *rejoice* in Him, who rules by His might *forever*, whose eyes keep watch on the nations—let not the rebellious exalt themselves."

Psalm 66:5-7 (ESV)

God in Heaven, as we reflect on just one example of how You provided for Your people, please keep the eyes of these leaders fixed on You as they do their daily work for the people of Kentucky and our nation. We know that You placed each of these people in the role they hold for Your purposes. Grant them wisdom and humility. Amen.

Louisiana

US REPRESENTATIVES
Troy Carter
Garret Graves
Clay Higgins
Mike Johnson
Julia Letlow
Steve Scalise

US SENATORS
Bill Cassidy
John Kennedy

> "The ***plans*** of the ***heart*** belong to man, but the
> ***answer*** of the tongue is from the LORD."
>
> Proverbs 16:1 (ESV)

God, it is so humbling to be reminded how involved You are in the daily affairs of our lives. As these leaders from Louisiana take up their daily work, please keep their hearts laser-focused on the fact that they are providentially there for You and Your plans, not for their own plans and/or aspirations. You are so good to Your people, LORD. Amen.

Maine

US REPRESENTATIVES
Jared F. Golden
Chellie Pingree

US SENATORS
Susan M. Collins
Angus S. King Jr.

"For *kingship* belongs to the LORD, and He *rules* over the nations."

Psalm 22:28 (ESV)

Father, we pray for these elected servants from Maine. Please give them eyes to see and minds to understand this simple but deeply profound truth that You are ruling over all the nations. However, You are not ruling like a self-serving dictator. Rather, You allow the very people You created to lead and govern others. Help these servant-leaders to fully grasp their proper place in Your plan and always lead with You in mind. Amen.

Maryland

US REPRESENTATIVES
Andy Harris
Steny H. Hoyer
Glenn Ivey
Kweisi Mfume
Jamie Raskin
C. A. Dutch Ruppersberger
John P. Sarbanes
David J. Trone

US SENATORS
Benjamin L. Cardin
Chris Van Hollen

> "When a man's ways *please* the LORD, he makes even his enemies to be at *peace* with him."
>
> Proverbs 16:7 (ESV)

LORD, Your Word is so good! Thank you for constantly speaking to Your people in simple ways. Please guide these elected leaders from Maryland to not only understand this great promise from Proverbs, but also to put its message into practice each day. When their ways please You, even their enemies will be at peace with them. Amen.

Massachusetts

US REPRESENTATIVES
Jake Auchincloss
Katherine M. Clark
William R. Keating
Stephen F. Lynch
James P. McGovern
Seth Moulton
Richard E. Neal
Ayanna Pressley
Lori Trahan

US SENATORS
Edward J. Markey
Elizabeth Warren

> "Lying lips are an abomination to the LORD,
> but those who act *faithfully* are His ***delight***."
>
> Proverbs 12:22 (ESV)

Father God, it would be so easy to remain cynical about politicians lying. Distrust is rampant. So much so that we have built measurements like Politifact to assess the degree of dishonesty as True, Mostly True, Half True, Mostly False, False, and Pants on Fire. Please show us back to the clarity and simplicity of Proverbs 12:22. Guide these leaders from Massachusetts to execute simple honesty in their daily work for Your glory. Amen.

Michigan

US REPRESENTATIVES
Jack Bergman
Debbie Dingell
Bill Huizenga
John James
Daniel T. Kildee
Lisa C. McClain
John R. Moolenaar
Hillary J. Scholten
Elissa Slotkin
Haley M. Stevens
Shri Thaneder
Rashida Tlaib
Tim Walberg

US SENATORS
Gary C. Peters
Debbie Stabenow

"I lift my eyes to the hills. From where does my help come?
My *help* comes from the LORD, who made heaven and earth."

Psalm 121:1-2 (ESV)

LORD God in Heaven, we thank You for Your faithfulness for always being there for us. We humbly ask for Your presence and wisdom for these elected leaders from Michigan. Draw their hearts and minds to You as the only real source of help as they engage in their daily work for our nation. Amen.

Minnesota

US REPRESENTATIVES
Angie Craig
Tom Emmer
Brad Finstad
Michelle Fischbach
Betty McCollum
Ilhan Omar
Dean Phillips
Pete Stauber

US SENATORS
Amy Klobuchar
Tina Smith

"Be not wise in your own eyes; *fear* the LORD,
and *turn away* from evil."

Proverbs 3:7 (ESV)

As we pray for the national elected officials from Minnesota, we appeal to Your grace and strength for these leaders. Help them look to You first and to take Proverbs 3:7 seriously—to not be wise in their own eyes and to fear the LORD. Remind them each day that they are there to do Your work. Amen.

Mississippi

US REPRESENTATIVES
Mike Ezell
Michael Guest
Trent Kelly
Bennie G. Thompson

US SENATORS
Cindy Hyde-Smith
Roger F. Wicker

> "Let every person be subject to the governing authorities.
> For there is no *authority* except from God, and
> those that exist have been instituted by God."
>
> Romans 13:1 (ESV)

LORD, it is such a simple but profound truth that there is no authority except what has been granted by You. As we pray for these political leaders from Mississippi, please remind them that their authority comes only from You. As they meet, talk, propose, and consider legislation, keep their true responsibilities at the top of their minds, which is that they are in their respective positions because of and for You. Amen.

Missouri

US REPRESENTATIVES
Mark Alford
Eric Burlison
Cori Bush
Emanuel Cleaver
Sam Graves
Blaine Leutkemeyer
Jason Smith
Ann Wagner

US SENATORS
Josh Hawley
Eric Schmitt

"A fool gives full vent to his spirit, but a *wise* man *quietly* holds it back."

Proverbs 29:11 (ESV)

LORD, each elected official has been permitted to serve by Your authority alone. We fully acknowledge that You are working in the affairs of our national leadership to accomplish precisely what You want. As we pray for these leaders who represent the people of Missouri, help us all to remember the words of Proverbs 29:11 and mind our words. Guide these leaders to do their jobs with wisdom and represent You well in their work. Amen.

Montana

US REPRESENTATIVES
Matthew M. Rosendale Sr.
Ryan K. Zinke

US SENATORS
Steve Daines
Jon Tester

"Rejoice in *hope*, be *patient* in tribulation, be *constant* in prayer."

Romans 12:12 (ESV)

Heavenly Father, we are in a challenging time. It seems that people go out of their way to be fearful, pessimistic, and angry. We pray for these leaders from Montana (and for ourselves) to walk in the instruction of Romans 12:12. We know that You are faithful and we have many reasons to be hopeful. Please find us faithful in being constant in prayer for one another and for our nation. Amen.

Nebraska

US REPRESENTATIVES
Don Bacon
Mike Flood
Adrian Smith

US SENATORS
Deb Fischer
Pete Ricketts

"for God gave us a spirit not of fear but of
power and *love* and *self-control*."

2 Timothy 1:7 (ESV)

LORD, what a fantastic reminder of the kind of people we are meant to be, which is those who live not in fear but with power and self-control. May these words echo in the hearts and minds of the elected leaders from Nebraska. Help them to lead and serve with confidence and purpose, knowing they are there to do Your work. Amen.

Nevada

US REPRESENTATIVES
Mark E. Amodei
Steven Horsford
Susie Lee
Dina Titus

US SENATORS
Catherine Cortez Masto
Jacky Rosen

> "He has told you, O man, what is ***good***; and what does the LORD require of you but to do ***justice***, and to love ***kindness***, and to walk ***humbly*** with your God?"
>
> Micah 6:8 (ESV)

Almighty God, thank you for Your word and for this great passage in Micah. What a stunning reminder of how You expect us to live. We lift these leaders from Nevada and pray for their focus on doing justice, loving kindness, and walking humbly with You. Draw them to You as only You can. Amen.

New Hampshire

US REPRESENTATIVES
Ann M. Kuster
Chris Pappas

US SENATORS
Margaret Wood Hassan
Jeanne Shaheen

> "Who has spoken and it came to pass, unless
> the Lord has ***commanded*** it?"
>
> Lamentations 3:37 (ESV)

Father, from the beginning of time You have been speaking into and shaping the affairs of humanity. It is both humbling and reassuring that You are so intimately involved in our lives. Please guide these elected leaders from New Hampshire to fully understand that they have been placed, with purpose, in their positions by You and that You have appointed specific work for them to do for their state. Amen.

New Jersey

US REPRESENTATIVES
Josh Gottheimer
Thomas Kean
Andy Kim
Robert Menendez
Donald Norcross
Frank Pallone Jr.
Bill Pascrell Jr.
Donald M. Payne Jr.
Mikie Sherrill
Christopher H. Smith
Jefferson Van Drew
Bonnie Watson Coleman

US SENATORS
Cory Booker
Robert Menendez

> "Mark the ***blameless*** and behold the ***upright***, for there is a future for the man of peace. But transgressors shall be altogether destroyed; the future of the wicked shall be cut off."
>
> Psalm 37:37-38 (ESV)

Father in Heaven, You are very much a God of hope and faithfulness. We humbly ask that You fill these leaders who represent New Jersey with Your vision for peace. Help them to build relationships that bring glory to Your great name. We know that You are watching, and You care greatly about what happens in our government each day. Lord, help us. Amen.

New Mexico

US REPRESENTATIVES
Teresa Leger Fernandez
Melanie Ann Stansbury
Gabe Vasquez

US SENATORS
Martin Heinrich
Ben Ray Lujan

> "***Commit*** your way to the LORD; ***trust*** in Him, and He will ***act***."
>
> Psalm 37:5 (ESV)

LORD God, this is such a simple but profound promise. We lift these elected leaders from New Mexico. Help them see that Your ways are always best. Inspire them to commit, each day, their ways to You so they can lead well and become leaders that others want to imitate. Amen.

New York

US REPRESENTATIVES

Jamaal Bowman
Yvette D. Clarke
Anthony D'Esposito
Adriano Espaillat
Andrew Garbarino
Daniel Goldman
Brian Higgins
Hakeem S. Jeffries
Nick LaLota
Nicholas A. Langworthy
Michael Lawler
Nicole Malliotakis
Gregory W. Meeks
Grace Meng
Marcus Molinaro
Joseph D. Morelle
Jerrold Nadler
Alexandria Ocasio-Cortez
Patrick Ryan
George Santos
Elise M. Stefanik
Claudia Tenney
Paul Tonko
Ritchie Torres
Nydia M. Velazquez
Brandon Williams

US SENATORS

Kirsten E. Gillibrand
Charles E. Schumer

"So, whether you eat or drink, or whatever you do, do all to the *glory* of God."

1 Corinthians 10:31 (ESV)

Father God, we trust You and know that You hear our prayers. We humbly—but boldly—pray for these elected leaders from New York. Turn their hearts to You so they can lead and govern in ways that honor You. Help them to know that they are only in their positions because of You and Your plans. And Your plans, like Your timing, are perfect. Amen.

North Carolina

US REPRESENTATIVES	US SENATORS
Alma S. Adams	Ted Budd
Dan Bishop	Thom Tillis
Donald G. Davis	
Chuck Edwards	
Valerie Foushee	
Virginia Foxx	
Richard Hudson	
Jeff Jackson	
Kathy E. Manning	
Patrick T. McHenry	
Gregory Murphy	
Wiley Nickel	
Deborah K. Ross	
David Rouzer	

> "but they who **wait** for the LORD shall renew their **strength**;
> they shall mount up with wings like eagles; they shall run
> and not be weary; they shall walk and not faint."
>
> Isaiah 40:31 (ESV)

Father in Heaven, the daily pressures in life can be exhausting. For our elected leaders, it's certainly no different. LORD, help these leaders from North Carolina to wait for You as the only way to renew their strength. While the responsibility of their job is massive, please remind them that You selected them for these tasks at this time. Amen.

North Dakota

US REPRESENTATIVES
Kelly Armstrong

US SENATORS
Kevin Cramer
John Hoeven

"If you faint in the day of adversity, your strength is small."

Proverbs 24:10 (ESV)

Lord God, we pray for these elected officials who stepped up to represent North Dakota. Please renew their sense of purpose, Your purpose, every day. We seem to be living right in the middle of "adversity" each day. Guide these leaders to set examples for their colleagues—to live out what it looks like to lead with strength and conviction. Amen.

Northern Mariana Islands

DELEGATE
Gregorio Kilili Camacho Sablan

"Show yourself in all *respects* to be a model of *good works*."

Titus 2:7a (ESV)

Father, may this great encouragement be a guide for the Delegate for Northern Mariana Islands. By Your hand, he was chosen to do Your work in government. Help him to lead well and always be mindful that he is setting an example for others to follow. Amen.

Ohio

US REPRESENTATIVES
Troy Balderson
Joyce Beatty
Shontel Brown
Mike Carey
Warren Davidson
Bill Johnson
Jim Jordan
David P. Joyce
Marcy Kaptur
Greg Landsman
Robert E. Latta
Max Miller
Emilia Strong Sykes
Michael R. Turner
Brad R. Wenstrup

US SENATORS
Sherrod Brown
J.D. Vance

"Put away from you crooked speech, and put devious talk far from you."

Proverbs 4:24 (ESV)

Father God, as we lift these elected leaders from Ohio, we humbly ask that Your sense of integrity would flow through them in their daily work. Our current political environment seems so underhanded and toxic. As we read in Your Word, great movements often start with small groups. Help these leaders live out Proverbs 4:24 each day, and may this conviction be contagious. Amen.

Oklahoma

US REPRESENTATIVES
Stephanie I. Bice
Josh Brecheen
Tom Cole
Kevin Hern
Frank D. Lucas

US SENATORS
James Lankford
Markwayne Mullin

"See that no one repays anyone evil for evil, but always seek to do *good* to one another and to everyone."

1 Thessalonians 5:15 (ESV)

LORD, your Word often sounds very simple but is rarely easy to accomplish. Thank You for this great instruction. As we pray for the political leaders from Oklahoma, may these words stay squarely in focus in their daily work with other legislators and influencers. Amen.

Oregon

US REPRESENTATIVES
Cliff Bentz
Earl Blumenauer
Suzanne Bonamici
Lori Chavez-DeRemer
Val Hoyle
Andrea Salinas

US SENATORS
Jeff Merkley
Ron Wyden

"***Rejoice*** always, ***pray*** without ceasing, give ***thanks*** in all circumstances; for this is the will of God in Christ Jesus for you."

1 Thessalonians 5:16-18 (ESV)

Father in Heaven, we know that even though these words were written long ago, they have every bit as much relevance today as they ever have. Please encourage and inspire these elected representatives from Oregon to lead and live with these great words from 1 Thessalonians in mind. Draw these leaders to You and grant them humble wisdom. Amen.

Pennsylvania

US REPRESENTATIVES
Brendan F. Boyle
Matt Cartwright
Madeleine Dean
Christopher Deluzio
Dwight Evans
Brian K. Fitzpatrick
Chrissy Houlahan
John Joyce
Mike Kelly
Summer L. Lee
Daniel Meuser
Scott Perry
Guy Reschenthaler
Mary Gay Scanlon
Lloyd Smucker
Glenn Thompson
Susan Wild

US SENATORS
Robert P. Casey Jr.
John Fetterman

"Fear not, for I am *with* you; be not dismayed, for I am your God; I will *strengthen* you, I will *help* you, I will *uphold* you with my righteous right hand."

Isaiah 41:10 (ESV)

God, what a promise! As these political leaders from Pennsylvania take up their daily duties, please draw them to You for strength and help. In our current contentious political climate, help these legislators to not be dismayed or discouraged but rather to lean on You. Grant them faith and assurance that You are living and active—ready to help when asked. Amen.

Puerto Rico

RESIDENT COMMISSIONER
Jenniffer Gonzalez-Colon

> "The heart is deceitful above all things, and desperately sick; who can understand it?"
>
> Jeremiah 17:9 (ESV)

Heavenly Father, this passage from Jeremiah is a sobering reminder of what we are capable of without Your help and guidance. Please bless and guide the Resident Commissioner from Puerto Rico in her daily efforts to represent the interests of the territory she represents. Inspire her to look to and lean on You for direction. Amen.

Rhode Island

US REPRESENTATIVES
David N. Cicilline
Seth Magaziner

US SENATORS
Jack Reed
Sheldon Whitehouse

"Remind them to be submissive to rulers and authorities, to be *obedient*, to be ready for every *good work*."

Titus 3:1 (ESV)

Heavenly Father, we boldly pray for these leaders You called and appointed from Rhode Island. Keep their focus on You and help them to always remember that their positions are not by accident. Rather, You have very specific purposes in mind for each of them and the policies they will help to create. Guide them to lean into that truth each day. Amen.

South Carolina

US REPRESENTATIVES
James E. Clyburn
Jeff Duncan
Russell Fry
Nancy Mace
Ralph Norman
William R. Timmons IV
Joe Wilson

US SENATORS
Lindsey Graham
Tim Scott

"Indeed, if you call out for insight and cry aloud for understanding, and if you look for it as for silver and search for it as for hidden treasure, then you will understand the *fear* of the LORD and find the *knowledge* of God."

Proverbs 2:3-5 (NIV)

LORD, Your Word is full of promises for wisdom if we only ask for it. As we lift these political leaders from South Carolina, we humbly ask for them to be focused on You. The work ahead for our politicians is massive and challenging. Help these leaders fully grasp their role and daily look to You as the source of true and pure wisdom. Amen.

South Dakota

US REPRESENTATIVES
Dusty Johnson

US SENATORS
Mike Rounds

John Thune

> "First of all, then, I urge that supplications, prayers, intercessions, and thanksgivings be made for all people, for kings and all who are in high positions, that we may lead a ***peaceful*** and ***quiet*** life, ***godly*** and ***dignified*** in every way."
>
> 1 Timothy 2:1-2 (ESV)

LORD, this passage from 1 Timothy could not be timelier for our politicians and all of us. We pray these words specifically for the political leaders from South Dakota. As they enter their respective chambers each day for policy discussions, help them strive for peacefulness and godliness. Amen.

Tennessee

US REPRESENTATIVES
Tim Burchett
Steve Cohen
Scott DesJarlais
Charles J. (Chuck) Fleischmann
Mark E. Green
Diana Harshbarger
David Kustoff
Andrew Ogles
John W. Rose

US SENATORS
Marsha Blackburn
Bill Hagerty

"When *justice* is done, it is a *joy* to the *righteous* but terror to evildoers."

Proverbs 21:15 (ESV)

Father, we praise You for the encouragement that exists throughout Your Word. Also, we thank You for the warnings. May these called and elected leaders from Tennessee be mindful that You are always watching and listening. Help these leaders to always seek justice—Your justice—in their daily work. Amen.

Texas

US REPRESENTATIVES

Colin Z. Allred	Vincente Gonzalez
Jodey C. Arrington	Lance Gooden
Brian Babin	Kay Granger
Michael C. Burgess	Al Green
John R. Carter	Wesley Hunt
Greg Casar	Sheila Jackson Lee
Joaquin Castro	Ronny Jackson
Michael Cloud	Morgan Luttrell
Dan Crenshaw	Michael T. McCaul
Jasmine Crockett	Nathaniel Moran
Henry Cuellar	Troy E. Nehls
Monica De La Cruz	August Pfluger
Lloyd Doggett	Chip Roy
Jake Ellzey	Keith Self
Veronica Escobar	Pete Sessions
Pat Fallon	Beth Van Duyne
Lizzie Fletcher	Marc A. Veasey
Sylvia R. Garcia	Randy K. Weber Sr.
Tony Gonzalez	Roger Williams

US SENATORS

John Cornyn
Ted Cruz

> "Then the LORD answered Job out of the whirlwind and said: 'Who is this that darkens counsel by words without knowledge? Dress for action like a man; I will question you and you make it known to me."
>
> Job 38:1-3 (ESV)

Most High God, as we have seen in recent months in our nation, there are a variety of opinions about who is in charge. Each political party has been painfully guilty of abusing power that You have allowed them to have. As this chilling passage from Job indicates, You have always been and will forever be very much in control. We pray for these leaders from Texas to embrace their role each day as a true gift and honorable calling from You. Inspire them to remember that Your plan is in motion and they have been invited to participate. Amen.

Utah

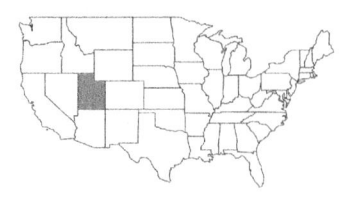

US REPRESENTATIVES
John R. Curtis
Blake D. Moore
Burgess Owens
Chris Stewart

US SENATORS
Mike Lee
Mitt Romney

"***Blessed*** is the man who walks not in the counsel of the wicked, nor stands in the way of sinners, nor sits in the seat of scoffers; but his ***delight*** is in the ***law*** of the LORD, and on His law he meditates day and night. He is like a tree planted by streams of water that yields its fruit in its season, and its leaf does not wither. In all that he does, he ***prospers***. The wicked are not so, but are like chaff that the wind drives away."

Psalm 1:1-4 (ESV)

Gracious LORD, we pray for the political leaders from Utah to remember this Psalm in their daily work—as we ask the same for ourselves. It is often quite easy to sit in judgment of those with whom we disagree—to the point of scoffing at them for their differing opinion. Your words are amazingly timely! Please help these leaders (and us) to learn to truly "delight in the law of the LORD." Amen.

Vermont

US REPRESENTATIVES
Becca Balint

US SENATORS
Bernard Sanders

Peter Welch

"For You *formed* my inward parts; you knitted me together in my mother's womb. I *praise* you, for I am *fearfully* and *wonderfully* made."

Psalm 139:13-14 (ESV)

Father God, this beautiful truth is so simple. Thank you for creating us precisely how you created us. As we pray for these elected representatives from Vermont, we boldly ask that Your truths, such as the one declared in Psalm 139:13-14, would be alive and considered in their daily discussions. We know that You don't need anyone in particular in government. Rather, You have permitted each elected person to be in their roles for Your divine purposes. We praise You for what You will accomplish. Amen.

U.S. Virgin Islands

DELEGATE
Stacey E. Plaskett

"For my ***thoughts*** are not your thoughts, neither are your ways my ***ways***, declares the LORD."

Isaiah 55:8 (NIV)

Almighty God, thank You for the simple truth of Isaiah 55:8. Your ways are vastly different from ours. We pray for the Delegate from the U.S. Virgin Islands to embrace this truth and lean into what You want to accomplish through her service. Thank you for Your mercy and patience with us. Amen.

Virginia

US REPRESENTATIVES
Donald S. Beyer Jr.
Ben Cline
Gerald E. Connolly
Bob Good
H. Morgan Griffith
Jennifer A. Kiggans
Jennifer L. McClellan
Robert C. (Bobby) Scott
Abigail Davis Spanberger
Jennifer Wexton
Robert Wittman

US SENATORS
Tim Kaine
Mark R. Warner

> "Search me, O God, and know my **heart**! Try me and know my **thoughts**! And see if there be any grievous way in me, and **lead** me in the way everlasting!"
>
> Psalm 139:23-24 (ESV)

LORD God, often the pleas and prayers in Scripture are so intimate that it is difficult for us to say those same words to You. Psalm 139:23-24 is such a passage. You certainly do not need our permission to search our hearts or to know our thoughts; You created us. We pray that these truths would weave themselves into the minds of the political leaders from Virginia. May they work each day with an increasing knowledge that You know their motives. Lead them (and us) in the way everlasting. Amen.

Washington

US REPRESENTATIVES
Suzan K. DelBene
Pramila Jayapal
Derek Kilmer
Rick Larsen
Cathy McMorris Rodgers
Dan Newhouse
Marie Glussenkamp Perez
Kim Schrier
Adam Smith
Marilyn Strickland

US SENATORS
Maria Cantwell
Patty Murray

> "The fool says in his heart, 'There is no God.' They are corrupt, they do abominable deeds; there is none who does good."
>
> Psalm 14:1 (ESV)

Oh God, forgive us for living, working, and leading like You don't care or are not even real. We boldly but humbly ask for You to make Yourself undeniably "real" for these political leaders from Washington. Help them to clearly see that You are not only very real but also that You unconditionally love each one of them and care greatly for the work that you have for them to do. You care so much that You placed each one of them specifically in their roles in government. Help them to lead with that incredible truth in mind. Amen.

West Virginia

US REPRESENTATIVES
Carol D. Miller
Alexander X. Mooney

US SENATORS
Shelley Moore Capito
Joe Manchin III

"For the wrath of God is revealed from heaven against all ungodliness and unrighteousness of men, who by their unrighteousness suppress the *truth*.

For what can be known about God is plain to them, because God has shown it to them. For His invisible attributes, namely, his ***eternal power*** and ***divine nature,*** have been clearly perceived, ever since the creation of the world, in the things that have been made. So they are without excuse."

Romans 1:18-20 (ESV)

LORD, we thank You for how plainly You have revealed Yourself. Your fingerprints are everywhere—if we would simply open the eyes that You created in us and look around. We lift up these elected leaders from West Virginia. Guide them to lead in the truth that we are all stewards of time, trust, and knowledge of You. Help them to boldly lead, always with Your purposes in mind. Amen.

Wisconsin

US REPRESENTATIVES
Scott Fitzgerald
Mike Gallagher
Glenn Grothman
Gwen Moore
Mark Pocan
Bryan Steil
Thomas P. Tiffany
Derrick Van Orden

US SENATORS
Tammy Baldwin
Ron Johnson

"Pride goes before destruction, and a haughty spirit before a fall."

Proverbs 16:18 (ESV)

God in Heaven, You see every thought and every motive in our hearts. Please remind the elected leaders from Wisconsin to be humble in how they conduct their citizens' business each day. Keep their motives pure and pointed to You. News of the day is full of this Proverb proving itself true, which is that pride comes before a fall. Help these leaders and all of us to remember this profound warning and conduct our lives accordingly, with Your help. Amen.

Wyoming

US REPRESENTATIVES
Harriet Hageman

US SENATORS
John Barrasso

Cynthia M. Lummis

"You will *seek* me and *find* me, when you seek me with all your *heart*."

Jeremiah 29:13 (ESV)

Great God in Heaven, thank You for the simple fact that finding You is not a mystery. You are here. As we pray for these political leaders from Wyoming, we pray that their thoughts, motives, and relationships reflect Your love and wisdom. Help them to always be seeking You, and fully understanding that You can be found and relied upon to help with anything they face. Amen.

Acknowledgments

We serve an amazing **God**. I want to thank Him first. After a great deal of prompting on God's part and super-human stubbornness on my part, this project finally saw the light of day.

Next, I am profoundly grateful for the support and encouragement from **my wonderful wife, Marte**. She has been a sounding board, critic, test audience, and overall cheerleader through this entire process.

Our superb children, Ellie and Matt, have also been a tremendous source of inspiration. They make me want to get better...always and in everything.

I owe **Pastor Willy Rice from Calvary Church** in Clearwater, Florida a big thank-you. Every year in late November or early December, he does a sermon on 2 Timothy 4:21 which he calls, "Come Before Winter". Pastor Willy uses this text to encourage people to take action on what they KNOW God is prompting them to do. The central idea is no one is promised tomorrow so we all should do what needs to be done today. Don't procrastinate.

Finally, I would like to convey a sincere thank you to **my team at Two Penny Publishing**. From my initial connection with Jodi, the entire experience was intensely professional as well as deeply personal. They graciously made time for all of my bone-headed questions and encouraged me in each step of the writing process. They are the best in the business. Maybe I am a bit biased but, wow, what a terrific team!

Made in the USA
Columbia, SC
01 July 2023